VANGUARD SERIES

EDITOR: MARTIN WINDROW

THE 6th PANZER DIVISION 1937-45

Text by Oberst a.D. HELMUT RITGEN

with colour photographs by the author

OSPREY PUBLISHING LONDON

Published in 1982 by
Osprey Publishing Ltd
Member company of the George Philip Group
12–14 Long Acre, London WC2E 9LP
© Copyright 1982 Osprey Publishing Ltd
Reprinted 1984, 1985

ISBN 0 85045 453 0

Filmset in Great Britain
Printed in Hong Kong

Introduction

Even after the formation of the first three Panzer divisions in October 1935 the debate over the control, equipment and effectiveness of mobile and tank units continued. The strong cavalry branch—there had been three cavalry and seven infantry divisions in the Reichswehr—feared a decline in its influence after the breaking-up of all cavalry formations apart from one brigade. The resulting cavalry motorisation programme led to the build-up of three 'Light brigades', a fourth being formed after the Austrian Anschluss; these later became the 6th to 9th Panzer Divisions. They were based upon the organisation of the French *Division Légère Méchanique* and were intended to fulfil the traditional cavalry rôle of strategic reconnaissance and security, rather than prosecuting offensive operations.

The 1st Light Brigade was formed on 12 October 1937 at Wuppertal (Table 1). Its core was a truck-mounted infantry regiment of four battalions including a motorcycle battalion, and a two-battalion reconnaissance regiment with both

11th Panzer Regiment celebrates its first birthday, in the Sudetenland. Oberst Philipps stands in his command car, flanked by PzKpfw II tanks, behind the two battalion standards. (Author's collection, as are all other photographs published in this book.)

armoured car and rifle elements. A two-battalion artillery regiment, various supporting units, and a single battalion of 70 light tanks were incorporated; the latter had the capability for rapid movement by means of its own 'organic' tank transporters.

The infantry-minded German general staff also formed independent Panzer brigades as Army troops, to be allocated to support the infantry divisions with their horse-drawn transport. These brigades comprised two tank regiments each of two battalions. The second to be formed was 6th Panzer Brigade at Paderborn (Table 2).

As the staff allocation within 1st Light Brigade proved insufficient to control this difficult formation structure, the brigade was redesignated 1st Light Division in the spring of 1938, with only minor organisational changes. On the eve of the Sudeten crisis in September 1938 the division was

3

The 6th Panzer was the only division equipped with the Skoda-built PzKpfw 35(t). Weight, 10½ tons; crew, four; armour, 25mm front, 16mm side; ground pressure, 14lb/sq.in.; armament, 37mm L/42 gun with AP and HE ammunition, plus two Besa 7.92mm MGs; engine, 120hp at 1,200rpm. Note detachable rhomboid-shaped plate bearing the tank's tactical number.

moved close to the Czech border. The possibility of offensive operations underlined the weakness of the armoured component. Consequently 11th Panzer Regiment from 6th Panzer Brigade was attached to 1st Light Division, which thus became effectively a Panzer division during the subsequent 'Flower Campaign'—the occupation of the German Sudeten areas of Czechoslovakia which followed the Munich Conference.

In April 1939 at Prague the Wehrmacht took over numbers of Czech Skoda 35 tanks. These were immediately given to the 1st Light Division, and to the 11th Panzer Regiment, which was earmarked for this formation. The reliable Skoda, armed with a 37mm gun, became the backbone of 1st Light Division and of 6th Panzer Division—as 1st Light was redesignated after the Polish campaign, with 11th Panzer Regiment finally incorporated. The last of these tanks perished not far from Moscow in December 1941.

For the Polish campaign the division—the only armoured formation which was truly combat-ready—was equipped with a total of 221 tanks mounting 148 guns of 37mm and 75mm, a number unmatched by any other German division. It was first rushed to the Vistula east of Radom, and later fought near Warsaw.

During the 1940 French campaign the re-organized 6th Panzer Division (Table 4) served in Reinhardt's XXXXI Panzer Corps. It proved its efficiency and spirit during its strike across the Meuse towards the Channel coast, fighting its way 350km (217 miles) in nine days. It later advanced from the Aisne to the Swiss border.

After the French Armistice the German Panzer forces were re-organised, the tank establishment of the division being reduced and the total number of divisions doubled. Unlike most other formations, 6th Panzer Division received a slight increase in tank strength. The re-organised rifle brigade would henceforward comprise two regiments each of two battalions, plus a motorcycle battalion—five infantry battalions, as against three of tanks. The artillery regiment was permanently given a third (medium) battalion. This organisation set a pattern for the next

A roadblock of trams erected during the Polish defence of Warsaw, September 1939.

chapter in the history of the Panzer divisions (Table 5).

The character and tactics of the Panzer war were changed dramatically in Russia in 1941 by the unexpected appearance of the Soviet T-34 and KV-1 tanks. Nevertheless 6th Panzer Division, now serving in 4th Panzer Group, succeeded in advancing to the outskirts of two different 'capitals'—Leningrad, and later Moscow. December 1941 found the division on the Volga/Moscow Canal, facing extreme cold, fresh Siberian reserves, and the exhaustion of a long and unremitting advance. A severe crisis gripped the German forces, which had now lost most of their artillery and nearly all their tanks through enemy action and, more devastating still, mechanical failure in the extreme physical conditions. The surviving members of 6th Panzer Division fought as infantry during a most punishing retreat; but soon afterwards regained the initiative in the 'Snail Offensive' north of Smolensk, despite the terrible cold. In April 1942 the division was relieved and sent to France to recuperate.

In November 1942 the refreshed and totally re-equipped division (Table 6) returned to Russia,

One of the division's few PzKpfw IV Ausf.B tanks—which equipped only one platoon per battalion—burnt out after taking several hits from Polish anti-tank guns near Warsaw; the commander, Prince Ratibor, was killed.

now with about 160 tanks, mostly PzKpfw III and IV models. It de-trained south of Stalingrad, which had just been encircled by the Soviet counter-offensive. By skilful manoeuvre the division succeeded in driving a deep wedge into the Soviet covering force, penetrating to within 48km (29 miles) of Stalingrad before being halted. When it was ordered to fall back in order to halt the Soviet offensive between the Don and the Donets, the diminishing number of tanks and the improved Soviet tactics forced upon 6th Panzer Division a new type of organization. An improvised 'Panzerkampfgruppe'—'Armoured Battle Group'—concentrated all remaining tanks, APCs and armoured artillery, often of several divisions, into a mobile force led by a regimental commander. Elements of the division served first in Kampfgruppe von Huenersdorff and later in Kampfgruppe Bäke; their mobile defensive operations led eventually to the recapture of Kharkov and Belgorod.

The Krupp-'Protz-KW' 6 × 4 truck, powered by the same four-cylinder air-cooled engine as the PzKpfw Ia tank (60hp/2,500rpm), was the transport for the bulk of the division's motorised infantry. The rear view shows the 4th Cavalry Rifle Regt. on the march.

Once again the division was refitted, minus one tank battalion which was sent back to Germany to train with the new PzKpfw V Panther. 6th Panzer Division took part in the futile Operation 'Citadel', the pincer-movement on the Kursk Salient in July 1943. From then until summer 1944 the division fought its way back to the west, always at focal points of the stubborn defensive operations of Army Group South.

After a short recuperation in Germany the division was sent in July 1944 to East Prussia for the mobile defence of the eastern borders of the Reich. These operations lasted until November; in December 6th Panzer Division moved to Hungary, fighting there until March 1945. In April it defended Vienna, and ended the war in Czechoslovakia. Most of the surviving soldiers surrendered to the US 3rd Army; nevertheless they were handed over to the Soviets, and their captivity did not end until 1955.

The division was led by a number of outstanding officers, most of them ex-cavalrymen. Among them were Generaloberst Hoepner (executed 1944), Generaloberst Raus, Generalmajor von Huenersdorff (killed in action July 1943), and Generalleutnant von Waldenfels. One of its 1st General Staff Officers was Count von Kielmansegg, later C-in-C AFCENT (NATO).

It was natural that this cavalry-sponsored division should attract the attention of officers involved in the resistance to Hitler. It is said that during the deployment for the Sudeten occupation the divisional commander, Hoepner, planned Hitler's arrest and the disarmament of his bodyguard: but the outcome of the Munich Conference rendered the plan impossible. The division's 2nd General Staff Officer between 1938 and 1941 was none other than Count von Stauffenberg, the man who actually placed the bomb in the vain assassination attempt of 20 July 1944. Generalmajor von Huenersdorff, who was killed tragically early, was another fanatical opponent of Hitler.

The division's losses in action were high. Up to May 1945 they amounted to 7,068 dead; 24,342 wounded; and 4,230 missing. Despite its casualties, despite the indescribable stress of many of its campaigns, and despite the hopeless situations in which it was caught on more than one occasion, its resilience and flexibility were astonishing. The 6th Panzer Division held together, and never lost its spirit.

1937–40

Formation, and 'Flower Campaign', 1937–38

Most of the units which later made up the 6th Panzer Division had been formed by October 1937: the 1st Light Brigade at Wuppertal under Generalmajor Hoepner, and the 11th Panzer Regiment at Paderborn under command of 6th Panzer Brigade. The former was under XV Corps, the latter, VI Corps. Spring 1938 saw the 1st Light Brigade redesignated as a division. For the originally envisaged rôle of strategic reconnaissance and security its mainstay was the rifle regiment of four battalions including one motor-cycle battalion. The regiment was redesignated as a Kavallerieschützenregiment in 1938, its uniforms being distinguished by cavalry-yellow Waffenfarbe. The motorcycle battalion later became the independent 6th Motorcycle Battalion. The regiment also incorporated the 17 (Kraftfahrzeug-Geschütz) Kompanie, a support company with 12 short-barreled 75mm guns. All the rifle companies had twice the allocation of machine guns of foot infantry companies; they were fully motorised, being mounted in Krupp-Protz-Kw 'soft-skin' transport.

The 6th Recce Regiment was soon reduced to 6th Recce Battalion, incorporating both armoured car and rifle companies.

The independent 65th Panzer Battalion, with an HQ and three companies, had a total strength of some 70 PzKpfw I and II light tanks armed with machine guns and 20mm cannon. They had their own tank transporters, 9-ton Buessing 6 × 4 trucks with low-loader trailers which served as loading ramps. The battalion could thus move fast by road.

The 75mm infantry howitzer was the main integral support weapon of the Panzer-Grenadier regiments; it was later replaced by the 150mm infantry gun.

The 76th Artillery Regiment comprised an HQ, and two motorised battalions each armed with 12 105mm light field howitzers drawn by half-track prime movers. The 41st Tank Destroyer Battalion had nothing but 37mm anti-tank guns at this date.

The mainstay of the divisional artillery was the 105mm light field howitzer M.18; this early model lacks a muzzle-brake.

Divisional vehicles speeding through a Belgian road-block in the Ardennes, 1940.

Monthermé, scene of the Meuse crossing of 15 May 1940. The far slopes are under artillery fire.

The 11th Panzer Regiment—not yet attached to 1st Light Division—comprised an HQ and two battalions, each of them with an HQ, two light and one medium tank companies. Each company had 22 PzKpfw I and II tanks, but the medium companies had PzKpfw IVs in the fourth of their five-tank platoons.

The actual strength of the division was thus far from impressive. The PzKpfw Ia (Krupp) and Ib (Maybach) represented the mass of its tanks. Not only were these vehicles light (5.3 tons), thinly armoured (maximum 15mm) and lightly armed (two 7.92mm machine guns), they were also very unreliable. The Krupp-built model suffered from overheating of its air-cooled engine and its steering-brakes, and from shedding tracks. Nevertheless the two-man crews were very proud of these 'beasts', even though they often coughed and spluttered to a halt when rattling along the road. This meant dismounting, opening the access-hatches, and trying to start them up again. Changing the spark-plugs or operating the fuel pump by hand—at the cost of blackened, burnt and bruised fingers and faces—sometimes got the 'beast' started again with a loud bang; otherwise it was ignominiously taken away by the recovery team.

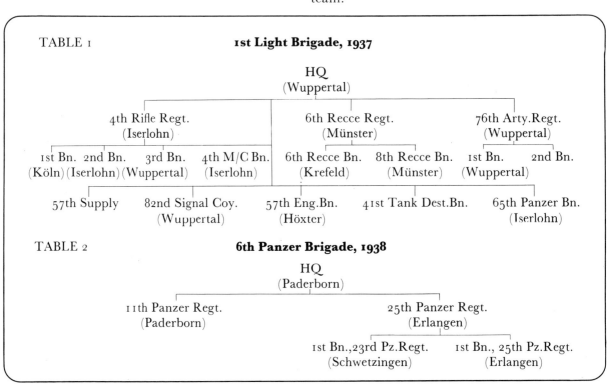

TABLE 1 — **1st Light Brigade, 1937**

HQ (Wuppertal)

- 4th Rifle Regt. (Iserlohn)
  - 1st Bn. (Köln)
  - 2nd Bn. (Iserlohn)
  - 3rd Bn. (Wuppertal)
  - 4th M/C Bn. (Iserlohn)
  - 57th Supply
  - 82nd Signal Coy. (Wuppertal)
- 6th Recce Regt. (Münster)
  - 6th Recce Bn. (Krefeld)
  - 8th Recce Bn. (Münster)
  - 57th Eng.Bn. (Höxter)
  - 41st Tank Dest.Bn.
- 76th Arty.Regt. (Wuppertal)
  - 1st Bn. (Wuppertal)
  - 2nd Bn.
  - 65th Panzer Bn. (Iserlohn)

TABLE 2 — **6th Panzer Brigade, 1938**

HQ (Paderborn)

- 11th Panzer Regt. (Paderborn)
- 25th Panzer Regt. (Erlangen)
  - 1st Bn.,23rd Pz.Regt. (Schwetzingen)
  - 1st Bn., 25th Pz.Regt. (Erlangen)

A Skoda 35 tank company of 11th Pz.Regt. wait in a wood near Mayen for the opening of the *blitzkrieg* **on France: April 1940.**

Although the PzKpfw II, with its armament of a 20mm cannon and a machine gun, and its three-man crew including a radio operator, was more reliable than the PzKpfw I, it was still far from perfect. Oberst Philipps, the very able CO of 11th Panzer Regiment, who had played a part in tank development at OKH before his assignment to the unit, comforted his officers after 40 per cent of the tanks had broken down on a normal road march with the assurance that information had been received that the British Mobile Division had suffered a higher break-down rate during a similar march the previous week!

In September 1938 Hitler had demanded the transfer of the Sudeten-German areas from Czechoslovakia to the Reich. On the pretext of 'autumn manoeuvres' the 1st Light Division and 11th Panzer Regiment were moved first to Saxony, and then up to the Czech frontier. The *coup d'état* which Generalmajor Hoepner is said to have planned against Hitler at this date must seem, in retrospect, to have stood little chance of success. The officers were certainly conservative, but traditional loyalty to the sovereign had in some measure been transferred to the Führer. The integrity of the officer corps had been shaken by Hitler's shrewd dismissals of the C-in-Cs von Blomberg and von Fritsch. The majority of the other ranks had been indoctrinated with Hitler Youth ideals; they were ardent soldiers, but not against their national leader. In fact not even the regimental commanders were taken into the general's confidence in this matter.

One day after the Munich Conference the 11th Panzer Regiment was temporarily attached to the 1st Light Division, which thus became an under-strength Panzer division. On 4 October the division crossed the frontier and during the next few days was exuberantly welcomed by the German-speaking population of the newly occupied areas. These few days of the 'Flower Campaign' near Pilsen—with its excellent beer!—did wonders for the pride and confidence of the units involved.

During the winter of 1938–39 training continued. The 1st Light Division was not among the units which occupied the rest of Czechoslovakia in March 1939. In mid-April about 130 Skoda 35 light tanks (designated in German service PzKpfw 35(t), the 't' standing for *tscheshich*) arrived at Paderborn for the 11th Panzer Regiment and 65th Panzer Battalion. Armed with an MV738ms 37mm gun and two Besa 7.92mm machine guns, this fine and reliable offspring of the Vickers 6-ton tank was designed as an infantry support vehicle

9

TABLE 3

**Light Tank Company,
11th Pz.Regt., 1937–38**

HQ
1 × PzBefw I
1 × PzKpfw I

Platoon	*Platoon*	*Platoon*	*Platoon*
1 × PzKpfw II	1 × PzKpfw II	1 × PzKpfw II	5 × PzKpfw II
4 × PzKpfw I	4 × PzKpfw I	4 × PzKpfw I	

**Light Tank Company,
11th Pz.Regt., 1939–41**

HQ
2 × PzKpfw 35(t)

Platoon	*Platoon*	*Platoon*	*Platoon*
5 × PzKpfw 35(t)	5 × PzKpfw 35(t)	5 × PzKpfw 35(t)	5 × PzKpfw II

**Light Tank Company,
11th Pz.Regt., 1942–43**

HQ
2 × PzKpfw III
(50mm L/60)

Platoon	*Platoon*	*Platoon*	*'Lt.Platoon'*
5 × PzKpfw III	5 × PzKpfw III	5 × PzKpfw IIIN	5 × PzKpfw II
(50mm L/60)	(50mm L/60)	(75mm L/24)	*(Not issued)*

The division pours across the plain of Champagne.

with a three-man crew. The OC 11th Panzer Regiment ordered that it should be manned by four men, adding a loader (without seat or observation ports); German radios were also fitted. Considering the lack of Czech instructors or technical manuals, training progressed surprisingly fast to the stage of range firing. In July it was decided to discard all PzKpfw I tanks and some of the PzKpfw IIs. The division, together with the 11th Panzer Regiment, now fielded a tank regiment of three battalions each with an HQ, one medium and two light companies, totalling 65 PzKpfw II, 114 Skoda PzKpfw 35(t) and 42 PzKpfw IV—221 tanks in all.

No other Panzer regiment of that date could match this number of guns. This level of equipment marked a change from the previous philosophy of massed tank attacks in the framework of a brigade of more than 400 light vehicles advancing through the infantry in order to penetrate a position and saturate the opposing anti-tank defences.

In 1939 the formation of the 6th Rifle Brigade marked the re-organisation of the divisional infantry. The brigade consisted henceforward of the 4th Cavalry Rifle Regiment with an HQ three rifle battalions and one support gun company, and the 6th Motorcycle Battalion (the former 4th

Noon, 26 May 1940: the division's tanks advance to attack Cassel (background), defended by the British 145th Brigade; a PzKpfw II follows Skodas—note air recognition flags, and the detachable tactical number plate on the PzKpfw II, '502'.

Bn. of the rifle regiment). The infantry were still mounted in Krupp-Protz-Kw vehicles.

It should be noted that by this period the 65th Panzer Battalion had handed in its tank transporters, which had proved unsuitable both technically and tactically. While retaining its title, the battalion became in effect the 3rd Bn., 11th Panzer Regiment.

In mid-August 1939 the division left its

A crash-landed Ju 52/3m transport aircraft near St Omer; fuel for the advancing Panzer divisions was flown up in these machines.

The heavy casualties among the division's tanks at Cassel were mostly due to the accurate fire of British 17-pdr. guns sited in positions dug out of the walls.

garrisons and headed for Silesia, again under the pretext of 'autumn manoeuvres'. On 26 August it was assembled on the Polish frontier, ready for offensive operations.

Poland, September 1939

The German operational plan for the campaign in Poland called for the destruction of the Polish forces massed between Lodz and Warsaw by a double envelopment east of the Narew-Vistula line. The southern prong, formed by von Reichenau's 10th Army, would deliver the decisive stroke with its mechanised and armoured divisions. 1st Light Division, initially in Army reserve, followed XI Corps, and was committed to action when the infantry failed to break through the determined Polish defence. Under XIV Corps, and supported by air strikes, it penetrated via Wielun to the Warta River, and on 3 September it forced crossings in the direction of Lodz.

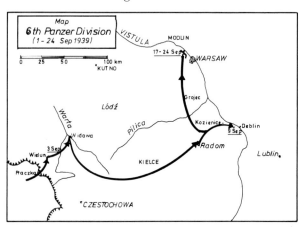

Owing to the deep, sandy soil of the dirt tracks and the limited cross-country mobility of the wheeled vehicles the river crossings took a long time. In these first days of the war the need for close co-operation between tanks and infantry was recognised. During the subsequent attack towards Widawa the 1st Light Division received a new mission: pursuit towards the Vistula to prevent enemy forces around Radom and Kielce withdrawing upon Warsaw. The objective was the Vistula east of Kozienice—an ambitious target. Within the next 50 hours the tanks covered 310km (192 miles) of a terrain resembling a desert: the fringes of the Lysa Gora mountains, via Radomsko, Wloszczowa and Radom. The spearhead reached the Vistula on 9 September. The Kielce-Radom Pocket—the first 'pocket' of the Second World War—was closed, and the 1st Light Division played a vital part in the capture of 60,000 men and 130 guns.

On 15 September the division came under XV Corps and was ordered north; a crisis had developed on the left wing of 8th Army. Strong Polish forces withdrawing from the west had attacked along the Bzura to the south in order to break through to Warsaw, which had been encircled. To prevent penetration of this encirclement from the east 1st Light Division was to bar the way across the Puszcza Kampinowska—a wooded heath between Warsaw and Modlin—by creating a wedge pointing towards the Vistula. This involved a difficult defence on two fronts in unsuitable terrain against superior Polish forces, who continued to attack with a fanatical courage born of despair. The situation became serious, and the division was forced to give up the river road between Warsaw and Modlin for a time. It has been reported that some 30,000 Polish troops from Kutno succeeded in reaching Warsaw at this time—though it helped them little in the long run.

On 21 September the division was relieved by infantry. While the fighting for Warsaw continued the division rested at Grojec. Although operations continued first at Warsaw and later between the Vistula and the Bug, the 1st Light Division prepared to go home. Losses had been 22 officers and 202 other ranks killed; 35 officers and 540 other ranks wounded; and 81 other ranks missing. Most of these casualties were suffered in the forest fighting near Warsaw. Few tanks had been lost. Co-operation between arms had been established; the capacities of the tanks had been recognised, but not, however, their limitations. Unnecessary losses had resulted from piecemeal commitment and from communication problems.

The morale of the returning units was high. They were ordered to prepare for new operations by 5 November. On 18 October 1st Light Division was redesignated 6th Panzer Division; 11th Panzer Regiment was incorporated, and 6th Panzer Brigade disbanded.

British PoWs are driven to the rear in one of their own lorries.

Victory in France, 1940

For many reasons Hitler was forced to delay his planned winter offensive against France, giving the tank units more time for training and maintenance. Late in January 1940 6th Panzer Division crossed the Rhine and assembled in the Euskirchen area west of Bonn. A month later it was transferred to the Westerwald. The crossing of the Meuse was practised several times on the Lahn River near Limburg. At the end of April all tracked vehicles crossed the Rhine once more to the Mayen area. There 6th Panzer remained at the outset of the German attack on France and the Low Countries on 10 May, not crossing the Luxembourg border at Vianden until 12 May. It is not widely known that XXXXI Panzer Corps, with 6th and 8th Panzer Divisions, crossed the Meuse at Monthermé at almost the same time as Guderian crossed further south at Sedan. The division had traversed the rugged terrain of the Ardennes mostly at night, in dry weather and without resistance, crossing three frontiers in 24 hours. At the Belgian border a captured Belgian officer watched in amazement as the tanks and other vehicles crossed a meadow near a blown bridge; it transpired that the field was heavily mined, but that the mines had been rendered inoperable by the wet winter. The division burst through the weak Maginot Line defences near Monthermé with artillery and Stuka support. On 15 May an engineer bridge was thrown across the Meuse; the advance guard set out, and at 2000 hours that night Montcornet, 65km (40 miles) west of the river, was taken.

6th Panzer Division now formed the spearhead of the German thrust across the Meuse. Thousands of French prisoners were sent marching towards Germany without guards. On the night of 16 May the division reached the River Oise at Guise. French armour counter-attacked vainly in the darkness; and the next morning bridgeheads were formed. The pursuit of the beaten French forces continued during the next few days. On 19 May General Giraud, C-in-C French 9th Army, was captured by a cook of a tank company. That night bridgeheads were secured across the Canal du Nord at Flesquières and Havrincourt on the old Cambrai battleground of 1917.

On 20 May a new enemy was encountered near Mondicourt; the British 36th Brigade held Doullens until nightfall. It was by-passed, and after a march of 100km (62 miles) the spearhead reached Rougefay, 20km from the coast. At the same time Abbeville was taken by the 2nd Panzer Division—the ring around the Franco-British Northern Armies had been closed. After a thrust

The graves of some of the gallant defenders of Cassel.

The formal reception of the 11th Pz.Regt., returning in triumph to its Paderborn garrison after the French campaign. Oberst Koll stands in the front of his SdKfz 15 staff car.

of 350km (217 miles) in just nine days, the 6th Panzer Division turned right on 21 May. Bridgeheads were established across the River Aa the following day against light resistance. On 23 May the division approached Cassel, HQ of General Lord Gort of the BEF. The attack planned for the 24th was ordered postponed, however: this was the famous 'stop order' which saved the BEF.

On 26 May the attack by the division towards Cassel was resumed, but by now the British had prepared the position for defence in order to gain time for their retreat to the sea. Cassel was a a fortress-like terraced hill, defended by the British 145th Infantry Brigade. Previous experience of the

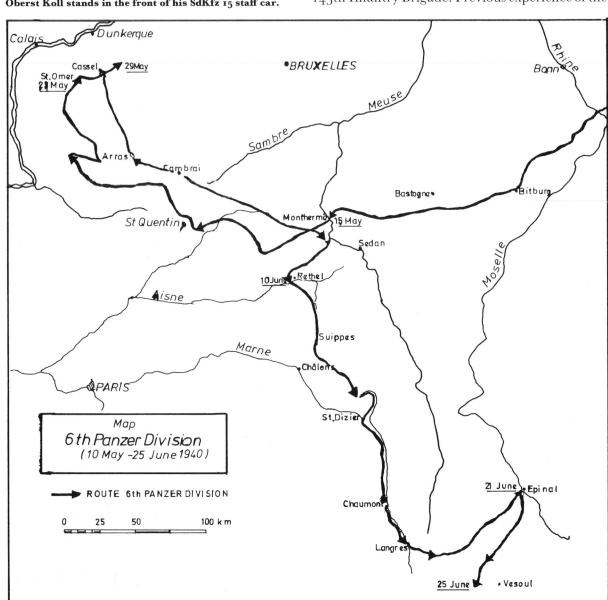

Map
6th Panzer Division
(10 May –25 June 1940)

ROUTE 6th PANZER DIVISION

0   25   50   100 km

Generaloberst Hoepner (left), former divisional commander and in spring 1941 the commander of 4th Panzer Army, visits his old unit. Generalmajor Landgraf (right) led 6th Panzer at this date; with him is his GSO 1, Major Count von Kielmansegg.

French led the tanks to be committed to attacks from the south and east without adequate infantry support: but this was a different kind of enemy, and heavy losses were suffered. At midnight the futile attack was abandoned. Kampfgruppe von Ravenstein meanwhile penetrated French fortifications on the Belgian border; but the order to retreat did not reach the Cassel garrison in time, and they continued to hold out. When the British defenders attempted a break-out on the night of 29 May they fell victim to Kampfgruppe Koll near Droogland. The brigade commander, 40 officers and nearly 2,000 men were captured. The next day 6th Panzer Division was relieved and sent south for a new phase of operations.

For this attack the division was assigned to Guderian's Panzergruppe, exchanging the 'K' (Kleist) for 'G' on the vehicles. The operation opened with the crossing of the Aisne near Rethel on 10 June; Perthes was reached that same night. The following day 6th Panzer Division crossed the Champagne battlefields of the First World War. The French forces conducted a stubborn series of delaying actions, holding on during the day with support from their strong and flexible artillery, and withdrawing to new positions by night. On 15 June the Rhine-Marne Canal was crossed, but the advance was halted by French Colonial troops. After a change of direction the division followed 1st Panzer Division more than 100km (62 miles) in one night, to Jussey via Langres. There 6th Panzer received a new order, to take the fortress of Epinal by *coup de main*. After severe fighting Epinal

and its forts finally surrendered on 21 June. On 25 June the Armistice formally concluded the campaign.

Re-organisation, 1940

The French campaign had finally established the Panzer divisions as the decisive element in ground warfare, and co-operation between the different arms within the division had improved. In August a major re-organisation of the Panzerwaffe began, and for this purpose 6th Panzer and 16th Infantry Divisions were 'coupled'. The latter was to become 16th Panzer Division; several units were exchanged between the two formations. While preparations for a possible invasion of England continued, the 6th Panzer Division took on its new shape.

The tank regiment had much the same shape and strength as at the beginning of the war, i.e. three battalions with HQs, six light companies each with 22 PzKpfw 35(t), and three medium companies each with 14 PzKpfw IV and five PzKpfw II—a total of 239 tanks counting the HQ sub-units at battalion and company levels, which

Oberst Baron von Seckendorff, the commander of 114th Rifle Regt., observes the battlefield from the top of a PzKpfw III command tank bearing the turret number '1107': Iamkino Station, July 1941.

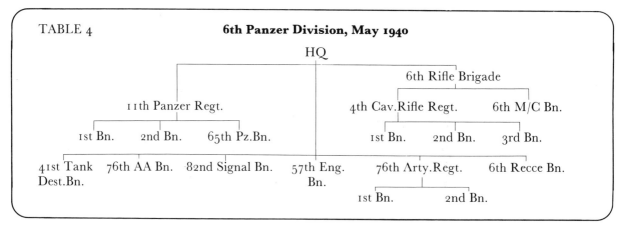

TABLE 4 **6th Panzer Division, May 1940**

					HQ					

```
                                    HQ
        ┌────────────────────────────┴──────────────────────────┐
   11th Panzer Regt.                              6th Rifle Brigade
   ┌──────┼──────┐                      ┌──────────────┴──────────────┐
1st Bn. 2nd Bn. 65th Pz.Bn.      4th Cav.Rifle Regt.            6th M/C Bn.
                                  ┌──────┼──────┐
                               1st Bn. 2nd Bn. 3rd Bn.

41st Tank   76th AA Bn.   82nd Signal Bn.   57th Eng.   76th Arty.Regt.   6th Recce Bn.
Dest.Bn.                                     Bn.         ┌──────┴──────┐
                                                      1st Bn.      2nd Bn.
```

The Skodas are supported by the PzKpfw IV tanks, which equipped one company of each battalion at this date. The small turret numbers—here '621'—seem to have been characteristic of the division.

Tank/infantry co-operation: Skoda '713' advances through a Russian village near Pskow, July 1941. Note heavy external stowage of fuel cans.

included 12 PzKpfw III command tanks, more suitable for such duties than the narrow-chested Skodas. The low tank production rate did not allow the replacement of the ageing and under-gunned Skodas despite their being declared no longer suitable for combat in spring 1941 by the Army Weapons Department (Heereswaffenamt). No replacements for these tanks were received before they met their end in front of the Moscow defences.

The three-battalion rifle regiment was increased to two two-battalion regiments by exchanging one battalion for a regimental HQ and two infantry battalions from 16th Infantry Division. Henceforth the 6th Rifle Brigade would consist of the 4th and 114th Rifle Regiments each with an HQ two motorised battalions and a support company with six 75mm infantry guns; and 6th Motorcycle Battalion. Only one rifle company received the new half-track armoured personnel carrier (Schützenpanzerwagen—SPW), a tiny step towards the mechanisation of the infantry.

The 41st Tank Destroyer Battalion received 15 50mm anti-tank guns, enough to re-equip one platoon in each company; the rest had to make do with the obsolete 37mm 'Doorknocker'. The 76th Artillery Regiment received a nominal increase by the addition of a 3rd (Medium) Battalion, but this had actually been attached since March 1940 anyway.

The period of celebration, and absolutely necessary maintenance work, did not last long. On 18 September 1940 the division left their garrisons and moved east, first to Deutsch Eylau and subsequently to Toruń and Kwidzyn in Poland. Training continued during the winter; deficiencies of vehicles and equipment in extreme cold were reported, but not remedied. A campaign in Russia was nothing but a vague and unpleasant possibility; a winter campaign was beyond the imagination. The possibility became less vague when officers received lessons in Russian, in particular the reading of Cyrillic script and maps.

The state of morale and training was high. Nobody wanted a war with the Soviet Union; but if war came, nobody was particularly bothered by the thought of the Soviet Army, which was believed to be 'far from a modern army' on the basis of its showing in Finland. Nevertheless, the idea of Russia's vast plains, poor communications and geographical character troubled most Germans: Napoleon's fate had not been forgotten.

1941–42

Towards Leningrad and Moscow

On 22 June 1941 6th Panzer Division crossed the German frontier near Tilsit, as part of the 4th Panzergruppe led by the former divisional commander, Hoepner. The army, supported by strong Luftwaffe elements, was to strike through the Baltic states on the far northern flank of the German invasion, aiming for Leningrad. From the first day the resistance was somewhat stiffer than had been expected, with Soviet border defences fighting stubbornly, and the Panzer IVs running out of ammunition before noon for the first time. Nevertheless all units took their objectives, and for the next few days they rolled north-east across Lithuania.

At Rasyeinyai the division was hit by a counter-attack by the 2nd Soviet Tank Division equipped with heavy KV-1 and KV-2 tanks. Armed respectively with a 76.2mm gun and a 152mm howitzer, these tanks had armour proof against anti-tank weapons up to 75mm calibre. The prototypes had been tried out during the Russo-Finnish War, and about 500 had been built by the outbreak of war with Germany; despite this, their existence was unknown to the Panzerwaffe, to whom they came as a considerable shock[1]. In an effort to stop these monsters two Panzer battalions and the anti-tank battalion concentrated their

[1] See Vanguard No. 24, *Soviet Heavy Tanks*

A PzKpfw 35(t) totally demolished by a Soviet bomb which fell into its open hatch.

fire, but without effect. Fortunately the Russian tanks were poorly led and their fire was very inaccurate; some even closed with the German tanks and rammed them. They were generally vulnerable to the German 88mm flak-gun, and some success was also achieved by rather desperate measures such as concentrating MG fire on the vision devices and turret rings to blind the crews and jam the turret race, and attacking their vulnerable points in close combat with petrol cans, grenades and high-explosive engineer charges.

That day changed the character of tank warfare,

The Soviet 'fast tank', BT-7-1 (with cylindrical turret), was a very mobile and reliable weapon in the armoury of the Red Army. Weighing 13¾ tons and mounting a 45mm gun, it had a 450hp engine and a crew of three; the suspension was the famous Christie design. Although versatile, it was of limited usefulness when in the position illustrated . . .

Highly 'atmospheric' snapshot of a roadside conference between elements of 1st and 6th Panzer Divisions during the advance on Leningrad, 1941. The SdKfz 221 and (background) 261 armoured cars belong to the reconnaissance battalion of 1st Pz.Div.; Oberstleutnant Siebert, CO of 2nd Bn., 11th Pz.Regt. briefs a despatch rider (left foreground).

as the KV represented a wholly new level of armament, armour protection and weight. German tanks had hitherto been intended mainly to fight enemy infantry and their supporting arms. From now on the main threat was the enemy tank itself, and the need to 'kill' it at as great a range as possible led to the design of longer-barreled guns of larger calibre. Tank guns of less than 75mm became more or less useless; and until HEAT ammunition was supplied in 1942 the L/24 75mm gun of the PzKpfw IV, with its low muzzle velocity of 385ms, was generally ineffective against the new Russian vehicles. The depth of the German Army's advance into Russia in 1941 despite this deficiency must appear something of a miracle.

The 6th Panzer Division overran every enemy position in its path, broke through the Stalin Line and crossed the River Dvina. Through dust and sand, woods and swamps it advanced via Ostrov and Pskov to the Luga River, the gateway to Leningrad—a trip of 800km (497 miles) in three weeks. At the Luga the advance came to a temporary halt to allow supplies and infantry to catch up.

The attack towards Leningrad resumed on 8 August. Against heavy resistance the division fought its way through strong field fortifications. In hard fighting 6th Panzer took the Duderhof hill south-west of Leningrad on 9 September. The splendid buildings and harbour of Leningrad were in sight—but in the meantime Hitler had decided not to assault, but only to invest the city. The 6th Panzer Division was ordered to join the offensive against Moscow on the central front.

The success of the thrust towards Leningrad was the result of able command decisions, excellent logistics and outstanding co-operation between all arms. The wooded and swampy terrain never allowed tanks to attack alone. Sometimes the division's infantry rode the tanks themselves; normally they rode their trucks and motorcycles between the tanks until they had to dismount and go into action. A forward battery of towed field howitzers followed close behind the spearhead

The BMW R12 motorcycle combination, a reliable machine used as a fighting vehicle early in the war. This one bears the divisional sign on the sidecar and the tactical sign of 2nd Bn.HQ, 11th Pz.Regt. on the mudguard. In the background, PzKpfw IV '600' and PzKpfw 35(t) '721'.

and deployed immediately into firing positions when required.

In August 1941 one change took place which was not at once recognised as important. Even during the last days of July single, unarmed vehicles of the division were able to travel without danger in unoccupied areas as far as the shores of Lake Peipus. They were often welcomed by a friendly population who regarded them as liberators from the Soviet regime, and who would exchange such things as butter and eggs for medical treatment. In August this situation changed abruptly. From then on growing numbers of partisans infested the rear areas, which soon acquired the character of a combat zone. German installations and vehicles were attacked; railways were torn up, roads mined, and raids were mounted by units of company size and more. The partisans also terrorised their own population to prevent their co-operation with the Germans. No soldier dared move in the rear areas or on furlough unless armed; vehicles had to be assembled in guarded convoys. This increased the bitterness of the war considerably.

On 2 October 1941 the 6th Panzer Division went into the attack once more, this time as part of Hoth's 3rd Panzer Army. For the breakthrough 11th Panzer Regt. was combined with the Skoda 38(t) tanks of 25th Panzer Regt., 7th Panzer Division into the temporary 'Panzer Brigade Koll'. The CO of 11th Panzer Regt. had under command about 260 tanks and a few APCs. The brigade achieved a deep penetration through enemy lines north of Vyasma, supported by strong Luftwaffe ground-attack elements under the command of General Wolfram von Richthofen. The next day the Dniepr River was crossed, and a few days later an encirclement of the Soviet forces opened the way to Moscow.

The supplies necessary for continuing the advance towards Moscow were brought up not only by road transport but also by 'Giant' gliders. However, the continuous autumn rain turned the dirt roads and tracks into bottomless mud; it must be remembered that metalled roads were ex-

The 50mm Pak-38 anti-tank gun was the most effective A/T weapon available to the division at the start of 'Barbarossa', and only 15 were issued. This one is photographed near Rasyeinyai, June 1941, with its 1-ton half-track prime mover and a Skoda 35 tank in the background.

tremely rare in Russia. The mud clogged everything, and weighed down boots, wheeled vehicles and tanks. All movements more or less stopped. Although elements of the division were able to reach their objectives—Kalinin, and points to the south—operations came to an effective standstill. The Soviets had a respite to complete their

German vehicles, including the horse-drawn supply wagons which still served in vast numbers in the infantry divisions, cross a bridge over a tributary of the Dniepr bearing a sign erected by 6th Panzer, which crossed on 3 October 1941. Advance through natural 'bottlenecks' was often seriously delayed by the fact that the mass of the German infantry still marched on foot.

fortifications, rebuild their forces, and assemble new formations by rail.

A mild frost hardened the ground again, and on 17 November the German attack was resumed. For the last time the division's few remaining tanks rolled eastwards; no replacements had been received since June. The Skodas were hampered by their pneumatic clutch, brake and steering controls, which failed in frosty conditions. Everyone was hoping to reach Moscow, and warm billets, before the hard winter set in. Although the troops were exhausted the attack gained ground. The neighbouring division on the left flank of 6th Panzer succeeded in forming a bridgehead over the Volga-Moscow Canal. The divisions to the right approached to within 30km (19 miles) of the Kremlin—but then the temperature fell to $-30°$ Centigrade. With the cold came snow, fog, and blizzards which restricted Luftwaffe support. The German forces lacked specialised winter equipment and clothing, and were paralysed by the freezing conditions.

At this moment the Soviets counter-attacked with fresh Siberian units, including armoured elements equipped with the excellent T-34, whose performance in deep snow was superior to that of the German tanks[1]. Without shelter or supplies

[1] See Vanguard 14, *The T-34 Tank*

the German armies were forced to withdraw. The 6th Panzer Division fought as rearguard for 3rd Panzer Army, which had only one axis for retreat. Thousands of German tanks, guns and vehicles had to be left behind. The very last tank of 6th Panzer, named 'Anthony the Last', broke down on 10 December near Klin, which was given up a few days later.

The division suffered the full rigour of the Russian winter without adequate equipment or training. Temperatures of below −30°C lasted for weeks, with deep snow-drifts rendering roads and tracks impassable. There were no snow-ploughs; and although every available pair of hands—German, and Russian civilian alike—was turned to shovelling the roads clear, motor transport became useless. Motor vehicles would not start unless warmed up first by improvised stoves, or by open fires which not infrequently got out of hand and burned the vehicle and adjacent buildings to the ground. Transport depended increasingly upon *panje*-sledges.

The supply of forward armoured units during speedy advances became a major problem due to the inadequate railway network and Russia's few and primitive roads. In October 1941 6th Panzer was partly supplied by means of Me 321 'Giant' gliders. These huge machines had a wingspan of 181ft.; a payload of 21½ tons was accommodated in a cargo bay the size of a railway freight wagon.

The *panje*—the tough little Russian peasant horse—became a most valuable possession; the once-proud 6th Panzer Division, now nicknamed by the troops '6th Panzer Division of Foot', had between one and two thousand of them, but hardly any serviceable motor vehicles. *Panje*-sledges were

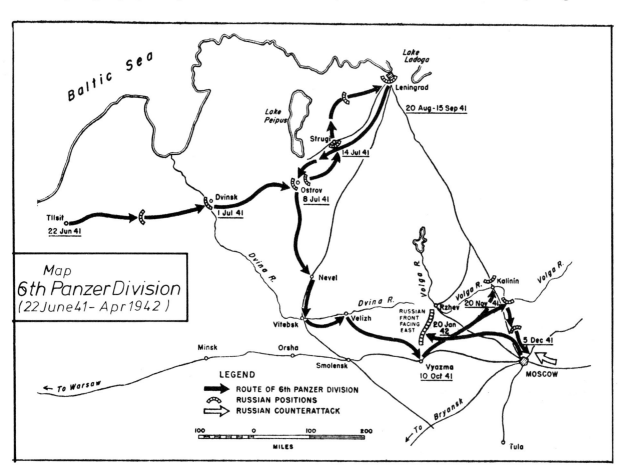

Map
6th Panzer Division
(22 June 41 - Apr 1942)

LEGEND
ROUTE OF 6th PANZER DIVISION
RUSSIAN POSITIONS
RUSSIAN COUNTERATTACK

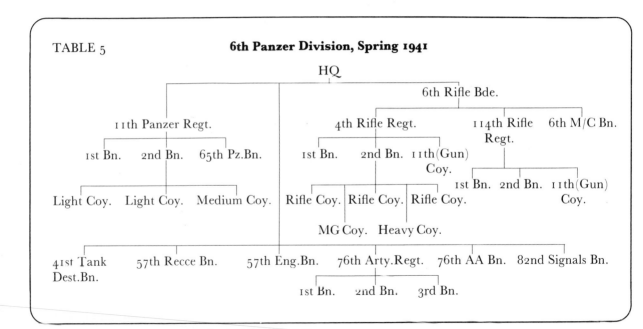

TABLE 5   **6th Panzer Division, Spring 1941**

HQ

- 11th Panzer Regt.
  - 1st Bn.
  - 2nd Bn.
  - 65th Pz.Bn.
    - Light Coy.
    - Light Coy.
    - Medium Coy.
- 6th Rifle Bde.
  - 4th Rifle Regt.
    - 1st Bn.
    - 2nd Bn.
      - Rifle Coy.
      - Rifle Coy.
      - Rifle Coy.
      - MG Coy.
      - Heavy Coy.
    - 11th(Gun) Coy.
  - 114th Rifle Regt.
    - 1st Bn.
    - 2nd Bn.
    - 11th(Gun) Coy.
  - 6th M/C Bn.
- 41st Tank Dest.Bn.
- 57th Recce Bn.
- 57th Eng.Bn.
- 76th Arty.Regt.
  - 1st Bn.
  - 2nd Bn.
  - 3rd Bn.
- 76th AA Bn.
- 82nd Signals Bn.

A signpost near Wolossowo in September 1941, showing the distances to Leningrad and Berlin-Central. At the bottom is the board of a 6th Pz.Div. supply company—'N' = *Nachschub*.

The autumn rains of 1941 transformed all roads into bottomless streams of mud, stopping the German offensive dead and over-stressing equipment which was already worn out.

used to move artillery pieces, ammunition, rations and wounded personnel. Even when the exhausted animals fell dead they were useful; they froze immediately, and within an incredibly short time would be stripped to the skeleton by famished passers-by, who sawed them up like a cake.

In an attempt to supplement the inadequate uniform clothing local workers were set to producing woollen sashes, waistcoats, ear muffs and mittens. Some fur garments and *valinki*—felt boots—were requisitioned locally, but the great majority of the men were without winter clothing until the results of the 'fur collection campaign' in the Reich reached the front in February 1942. Losses from wounds and frostbite were high; the wounded died of hypothermia, and of the strain of endless journeys back to hospitals which were themselves mainly understaffed and inadequately equipped. As discouraging was the failure of many German weapons to function in extreme cold, unlike Soviet equipment for which low-temperature lubricants were available. Machine guns did not fire, artillery pieces did not recoil, optics were covered with moisture and ice, and the hands of men trying to repair these faults froze to the metal.

To improvise the shelters which were necessary for defensive positions the engineers blasted craters in the hard-frozen ground. Covered with timber and protected by mines and obstacles,

TABLE 6

6th Panzer Division, October 1942

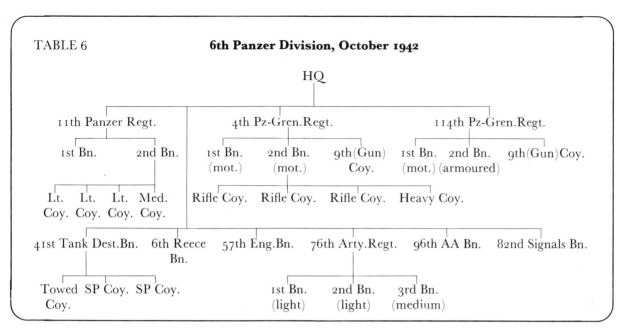

HQ

- 11th Panzer Regt.
  - 1st Bn.
  - 2nd Bn.
    - Lt. Coy.
    - Lt. Coy.
    - Lt. Coy.
    - Med. Coy.
- 4th Pz-Gren.Regt.
  - 1st Bn. (mot.)
  - 2nd Bn. (mot.)
  - 9th (Gun) Coy.
    - Rifle Coy.
    - Rifle Coy.
    - Rifle Coy.
    - Heavy Coy.
- 114th Pz-Gren.Regt.
  - 1st Bn. (mot.)
  - 2nd Bn. (armoured)
  - 9th (Gun) Coy.

- 41st Tank Dest.Bn.
  - Towed Coy.
  - SP Coy.
  - SP Coy.
- 6th Reece Bn.
- 57th Eng.Bn.
- 76th Arty.Regt.
  - 1st Bn. (light)
  - 2nd Bn. (light)
  - 3rd Bn. (medium)
- 96th AA Bn.
- 82nd Signals Bn.

these soon sent plumes of smoke into the air as the crews huddled in them round open fires.

When the division finally assembled its forces at the end of January 1942, it had less than 1,000 combat effectives and three artillery pieces. This assembly took place 70km (43 miles) behind the front between Smolensk and Vyazma. Soviet forces had penetrated the German line north-west of Rzhev with cavalry and sledge-borne infantry reinforced by paratroops and partisans. These forces threatened the German lifeline, the railway and road between Rzhev and Vyazma; the German 9th Army was in danger of encirclement and annihilation. A new front facing west had to be cobbled together from *ad hoc* units made up of survivors of decimated divisions, stragglers, supply train personnel, and others.

These units were used for a new type of offensive in which time was not important; the speed of a snail would be sufficient. This 'Snail Offensive' would advance only where it could find a worthwhile objective without incurring any danger, and would fall back into its 'shell' if rebuffed. The objective was to roll the enemy back to a distance of 15 to 30km from the vital artery of the *rollbahn*. After thorough preparation the first Soviet salient of three villages was taken by skill and surprise; these were immediately prepared for defence. One after another, villages in different sectors and at

General Model, then the commander of XXXXI Panzer Korps, with Oberst Koll of 11th Panzer Regiment, autumn 1941.

main text continued on page 26

The Colour Plates

The colour photographs on these pages are a small selection from a remarkable—perhaps literally unique—collection taken in 1940–44 by Colonel Ritgen during his front-line service. The camera was a Leica III (Summitar f 1.2 lens). Col.Ritgen's wife, at that time a nurse at the Paderborn military hospital, was a former employee of the Agfa company, and as a keen photographer herself was able to obtain through a personal contact with the firm a supply of the new and very rare Agfa 35mm colour film. The exposed films were sent back from Russia to Agfa through the Army mail service, and the processed pictures were kept in Germany by Frau Ritgen.

Col.Ritgen recalls that the excellent and sturdy Leica, which spent its time slung round his neck in a leather case, survived many hasty dives to the ground under Soviet shellfire; one one occasion he was forced to bale out of his burning PzKpfw III after coming off second best in an encounter with a KV-1, but the camera continued to function well. It had no built-in exposure meter, and given the circumstances Col. Ritgen was often limited to making a rough estimate, but it seldom let him down. It finally met its end in the stowage box of his tank near Tilly, Normandy in June 1944 when he was serving with the Panzer-Lehr Division. He was forced to take cover under the tank when caught by a heavy naval bombardment, and a shell splinter—probably courtesy of the cruiser HMS *Orion*—put paid to both stowage box and camera. Osprey are proud to have the opportunity of placing some of the remarkable results of Col. Ritgen's work before a wider public.

Front cover

PzKpfw IV Ausf.D tanks of 65th Panzer Battalion (in effect, 3rd Bn., 11th Pz.Regt.) photographed in East Prussia in May 1941 shortly before the invasion of Russia. The small turret number '421' identifies the battalion by its yellow colour, the company-'4', the platoon-'2', and the platoon leader's tank-'1'. The two yellow 'Xs' on the front plate beside the driver's visor are the divisional sign of 6th Panzer; this device replaced the original 'reversed Y' rune and two dots shortly before Operation 'Barbarossa'. The national cross is in plain white outline on the 'Panzer grey' paintwork. On the nearside trackguard may be seen the shielded driving- and head-lights, the fire extinguisher, a jacking block of thick timber, barrel cleaning rods, and four jerrycans held by a retaining bar marked with the divisional sign. Note open flap of ventilation port in turret roof: ventilator fans were not yet fitted.

A1, A2

Further views of the PzKpfw IVs of 65th Panzer Battalion in May 1941. The division had only three companies of these heavy support tanks at the time of the invasion of the USSR, the great bulk of the three tank battalions being made up of Skoda-built PzKpfw 35(t) tanks, with a few light PzKpfw IIs and some PzBefw.III command tanks. In the lower photograph an SdKfz 15 staff car in the foreground bears the tactical marking of divisional HQ on the mudguard. Two of the NCOs in the photograph wear white umpire's brassards, indicating an exercise; and the mixture of headgear worn by tank crews at this transitional period is also indicated—in this photograph may be seen the original black 'beret', the stop-gap field grey sidecap, and the new black sidecap.

B1

On the endless, sun-scorched steppes of northern Russia, Skoda-built PzKpfw 38(t) and German PzKpfw II tanks of 25th Pz.Regt. from 7th Pz.Div.; these were brigaded with 6th Pz.Div. tanks in 'Panzer Brigade Koll', led by the CO of 11th Pz.Regt., for the battles of October 1941.

B2

Photographed on 2 October 1941, during the break-through by Pz.Bde.Koll north of Vyazma: the brigade commander's PzBefw.III, with the white turret code 'RO6', on a typical Russian dirt road—*rollbahn*. In front of it, a column of Granit ambulances; to the right, Soviet prisoners; and in the background, smoke rising from an oil dump bombed by Stukas.

C1

A distant but fascinating photograph of the fighting of 2 October 1941, which repays close study. In the right foreground is a Soviet freight train overrun on the tracks—note two locomotives, one facing forward, the other to the rear. In the background several buildings are on fire, and the sky is black with smoke from an oil dump. In the left and centre background, PzKpfw 35(t) tanks in company strength may be seen advancing under fire.

C2

A column of armour from 'Pz.Bde.Koll' advance through woods past a burning Soviet ammunition truck; on the right, unguarded Soviet prisoners make their way to the rear. The leading PzKpfw 38(t) bears on the driver's visor the yellow 'Y' sign of 7th Pz.Div., identifying 25th Pz.Regt.

D1

Blurred but interesting shot of the division's second echelon passing through the supply convoys of the first echelon—the large number of vehicles visible in this photograph is a reminder of the enormous logistic 'tail' necessary to keep an armoured division moving. The PzKpfw 35(t) on the right carries an air recognition flag draped over the crew bedrolls on the rear deck. Note wooden stakes marking the edges of the *rollbahn*.

D2

Another view of Oberst Koll's 'RO6' on 2 October 1941, advancing towards a bridge in a typical Russian village. Modellers are recommended to study details of buildings and roadbed!

1▲

▼2

A

1▲

▼2

B

1 ▲

▼ 2

C

1 ▲

▼2

D

1▲

2▲ ▼3

E

1 ▲

2 ▲

▼ 3

F

1▲

2▲

▼3

G

1▲

▼2

H

The Colour Plates
(continued)

E1

Oberst von Grundherr, the divisional artillery commander of 6th Pz.Div., photographed in his heavily camouflaged command APC—note large frame aerial.

E2

Major (later Generalmajor) Dr.Franz Bäke, 1898–1978; this very gallant and distinguished officer, photographed here in 1943, held various appointments within 11th Pz.Regt. of 6th Pz.Div., and rose to command the regiment in 1943–44. During that winter he led the successful battle-group 'Heavy Panzer Regiment Bäke', whose Tiger and Panther tanks achieved extraordinary results in a number of engagements; and in 1945 he was promoted to commanding general of 13th Panzer Division. In this photo Maj.Bäke wears the black, pink-piped field uniform of the tank arm; the Knight's Cross with Oakleaves is worn at the throat—he was later awarded the Swords. On the left breast are the Iron Cross 1st Class; the gold Wound Badge, signifying at least five wounds in action; and the Tank Battle Badge. In his buttonhole are the Winter 1941–42 Medal ribbon and the ribbon of the 1914–18 Iron Cross 2nd Class bearing the silver eagle 'bar' for a subsequent Second World War award. Most striking of all, on his right sleeve are no less than three awards of the Tank Destruction Badge, for single-handed destruction of enemy AFVs with hand-held weapons at Kursk.

E3

October 1941: Oberst Koll, commanding officer of 11th Pz.Regt. and at that period the combined tank strength of both 6th and 7th Pz.Divs., in a confident pose in the cupola of his PzBefw.III—note detail of frame aerial. At the right is the CO's signals officer, wearing earphones. A pole aerial rises behind the Gefreiter standing at the left.

F1

Generalmajor Raus, formerly commander of the 4th Rifle Brigade, commanded 6th Pz.Div. from November 1941 to February 1943. He went on to command 4th Panzer Army from November 1943 to May 1944.

F2

Late summer 1941: a front-line conference at the forward HQ of 6th Panzer. *Left* is Generalmajor Landgraf, divisional commander from January to November 1941. *Second left*, in motorcyclist's coat, is Gen.Reinhardt, commanding general of XXXXI Panzer Corps until 30 September 1941. *Right*, in red-striped staff breeches, is the divisional GSO 1, Maj. Count von Kielmansegg, who rose after the war to general's rank in the Bundeswehr and commanded NATO-AFCENT.

F3

Cheerful divisional personnel pose with a wrecked Soviet T-28B tank in the first weeks of the Russian campaign. This 25-ton Russian derivative of the British Vickers A6E1 design was armed with a 76.2mm main gun and three MGs, and was first unveiled at a parade in October 1932. Note soldier clowning with 76.2mm round; and unidentified brigade and battalion markings on turret.

G1

The close support given to the armour by the ground-attack aircraft of the Luftwaffe is symbolised by this snapshot of General Wolfram Freiherr von Richthofen, the renowned Air Corps commander of the Stuka squadrons, after he had landed his Fi 156 Storch liaison aircraft for a front-line conference with Oberst Koll in autumn 1941. The fire of combat rises only 200 yards beyond. Just visible on von Richthofen's right forearm is the rare and prized cuff-title commemorating service with the First World War fighter wing commanded by his cousin, 'The Red Baron'. (For readers interested in uniform detail, see colour plate in Men-at-Arms 124, *German Commanders of World War II*.)

G2

The author collecting his lunch from a field kitchen mounted on the reliable 2½-ton 6 × 6 diesel lorry built by MAN, Henschel, Büssing-NAG, Magirus and Faun. The uncropped photograph shows, low on the right rear body of the truck, the white marking 'GI'— 'Gefechtstross I', 'forward battle-train'. Until 1944 each company had its own 'battle-train', including a field kitchen; subsequently these were incorporated into the supply companies of each battalion.

G3

Near the Don, winter 1942–43: the costly fighting following the attempt to open a corridor to the 6th Army trapped in Stalingrad. A wrecked Soviet T-34/76, with some of its ammunition spilled on the snow, is surrounded by curious Panzer-Grenadiers of 6th Pz.Div. dressed in the reversible winter combat suit.

H1

Oberst von Huenersdorff, CO of 11th Pz.Regt.—and of the division from February to July 1943—holds a front-line orders group during a January 1943 attack on the Soviet position known as 'Rabbit Farm'. During the costly fighting between the Don and the Donets that winter von Huenersdorff commanded an armoured battle-group of 6th and 7th Pz.Divs. and Army reserve assault artillery units.

H2

Between the Don and the Donets, winter 1942–43: in morning sunshine PzKpfw III tanks and SdKfz 251 APCs advance into a Russian village still burning from their tracer fire.

irregular intervals were captured. More than 80 villages were taken by the initiative of 6th Panzer Division.

Re-organisation in France, 1942

In April 1942 the division was transferred to Paris—after the Russian winter this was like being transported to fairyland. All personnel got leave, but training with new personnel and equipment

Winter was not kind to tanks. This PzBefw III of 6th Panzer has broken through thin ice into thick mud, November 1941. Unless dug out quickly it could be cemented to this spot for months to come by the imminent freeze-up.

began at once. 11th Panzer Regt. was to have two battalions only, each with one medium and three light companies equipped with PzKpfw IV Ausf. F2 and G and PzKpfw III Ausf. J and N. According to the table of organisation and equipment each company was to have an additional platoon of five light PzKpfw IIs, but in the event these were not supplied. The division's total tank strength was thus 160, against the 240 which it had fielded at the beginning of the Russian campaign. The 65th Panzer Bn. was disbanded and its light companies were used to fill up the other two battalions. As a temporary measure while awaiting the arrival of their new equipment, 11th Panzer Regt. were issued with French Somua S-35 (20 tons, 47mm gun) and Hotchkiss H-35/39 (12 tons, 37mm gun) tanks as an anti-invasion defence force.

The HQ of 6th Rifle Bde. was also disbanded. The two rifle regiments were redesignated as Panzer-Grenadier regiments; only one battalion—

2nd Bn.,114th Pz-Gren. Regt.—was equipped with half-track APCs. Each regiment received an infantry gun company with six 150mm howitzers in place of the 75mm weapons.

The 41st Tank Destroyer Bn. was equipped with 75mm L/48 Pak 40 guns—the same weapon as was mounted in the turret of the PzKpfw IV. One company received self-propelled guns on PzKpfw II chassis, the remainder were towed.

The 6th Motorcycle Bn. was amalgamated with 57th Reconnaissance Bn. to form 6th Panzer Reconnaissance Bn.; this combined-arms unit had both reconnaissance vehicles and Panzer-Grenadiers mounted in armoured half-tracks.

The 76th Artillery Regt. kept its three battalions, two equipped with three batteries each of four 105mm field howitzers (le.F.H.18) and one with three batteries each of four 150mm field howitzers (s.F.H.18). Self-propelled guns were not issued until spring of 1943. Generally, the mechanisation of the division had not made much progress since 1939.

In June 1942 the 6th Panzer Division was shifted to Brittany, near Rennes. The nearby Coetquidan training area enabled all units to fire their weapons and practise co-operation between arms. On 19 August 1942 the division was temporarily alerted when the Dieppe raid took place.

On 5 November a warning order for the return to Russia was received. During the subsequent period of preparation the Allies made their landings in French North Africa—Operation 'Torch'—and there was a temporary change of plan. All the division's tanks were mounted on rail cars, ready to roll down to the south of France—a more pleasant posting than Russia! But instead of locomotives there came confirmation of the move back to Russia, to begin on 14 November. This time 6th Panzer was better prepared for winter than it had been a year before; there was an issue of special winter clothing, heating devices for all vehicles, and so forth.

The rail movement was to follow two routes with the destinations of Stalino (Donetsk) and Belgorod. During the long trip up to the front there were numerous surprise attacks by partisans; an artillery commander and several men were killed, and many more wounded. On arrival in the Donetsk area the trains were re-routed to Moro-

The Soviets threw everything into the defence of Moscow—even dogs. This one was shot before it could run under a German tank, as it had been trained—note the vertical detonator rising from the mine strapped to its back.

zovsk and Kotelnikovo, the eastern terminals of the railway routes to Stalingrad. A difficult mission awaited the 6th Panzer Division.

The attempt to relieve Stalingrad

On 19 November strong Soviet forces had attacked and penetrated the long, weakly held flanks of the German wedge pointing towards Stalingrad, isolating the 6th Army under Paulus in and around the ruined city. The counter-stroke was to be delivered by von Manstein's Army Group Don, of which the strongest formation was the newly arrived 6th Panzer Division. Immediately after their arrival at Kotelnikovo the first units of the division had to go into action, destroying a brigade of Soviet armour and cavalry

A captured Soviet woman tank-driver.

By March 1942 German tanks had become very rare on the Eastern Front. This PzKpfw III with 50mm gun is neatly whitewashed, with repainted turret numbers '300'.

the encirclement. An extract from the Daily Report of HQ 4th Panzer Army, 2015, 21 December 1942:

'During the night of the 19th Colonel von Huenersdorff with the few remaining armoured elements struck deeply into the rear of the enemy. Overrunning the defences of Wassiljewka during the hours of darkness he forced the Myschkowa crossing. Crowded in a narrow spot, cut off from supplies of fuel and ammunition, he succeeded in holding the bridgehead for 36 hours against continuous enemy attack.'

★   ★   ★

The author remembers:

From the late morning of 19 December 11th Panzer-Regt. was engaged in attacks. The Soviets finally withdrew after prolonged, hard fighting, despite the deployment in this sector of Guards units. The tanks struggled forward through an area of ravines, treacherous obstacles with a thinly iced snow cover. They 'mopped up' the enemy in their fox-holes and destroyed their

(including one regiment equipped with camels!) before the attack towards Stalingrad could commence.

Against strong opposition the division succeeded in breaking through the Soviet armour covering

Winter 1941: the once-proud 6th Pz.Div. is now mobile only by means of *panje*-sledges. The author rides in the front of this one, muffled in a sheepskin coat and carrying an MP.40.

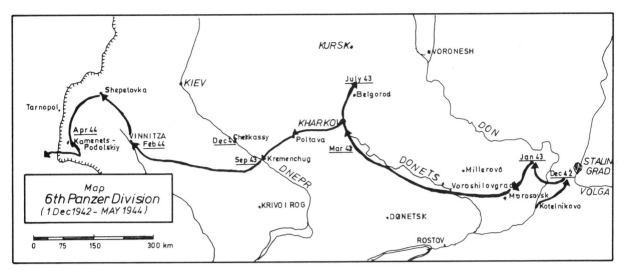

Map
6th Panzer Division
(1 Dec 1942 - MAY 1944)

0 75 150 300 km

remaining elements. In the clear sky Stukas circled, looking for targets ahead of the Panzer spearhead. Off to the left the recently captured village of Werchne Kumskii was crowned by mushrooms of smoke from shot-up enemy tanks. The CO, Oberst von Huenersdorff, stopped in line with the lead battalion on a hill feature when a message was received: 'New mission. Turn west via Hill 147 to Wassiljewka. Form bridgehead there.' After a

The welcome transfer to France in spring 1942 was followed by the re-equipment of the division. The three 'light' companies in each of the two tank battalions received the PzKpfw III Ausf.J with L/60 50mm gun, and a single platoon of Ausf.N tanks with the short 75mm howitzer. The 'medium' company in each battalion received the PzKpfw IV Ausf.F, with the L/48 75mm gun.

SdKfz 250/10 half-track with 37mm gun, as used by the division's reconnaissance battalion. The divisional sign and a tactical marking can just be made out painted on the top surface of the engine deck, forward of the hatches.

short study of the map he radioed an order to his units: 'Bring fighting to an end. Assemble on Hill E; come to orders group.'

According to intelligence reports an anti-tank position on Hill 147 was blocking the route to Wassiljewka. It was now 1330hrs, with the Russian winter sunset only an hour off. The situation was urgent if there was to be any hope of achieving the

The dash for the Myschkowa bridgehead: Oberst von Huenersdorff's command tank, in which the author rode during the attempt to drive a corridor through for the entombed 6th Army at Stalingrad, is seen in the foreground during the assembly of 11th Pz.Regt. on 19 December 1942.

mission that night. Fuel was short, as the supply convoy had not yet come up; but the enemy would certainly be reinforced the next day, and a delayed breakthrough would cost higher casualties.

Attacking with the westering sun at their backs the tanks rolled at top speed towards the enemy, their tracks throwing up glittering clouds of snow in the low, flat light. After crossing a road we came to a hill; this had to be Hill 147—and there was the enemy. 'Sand fountains' were splashing up, devilish close—one impact after another. The difficult ground delayed our charge; our guns replied to the Soviet fire, but the range was extreme and the targets were tiny and hard to make out. The defence included many 76.2mm anti-tank guns and anti-tank rifles. Several of our tanks were hit. Although some of the enemy guns were silenced, a further charge would cost unnecessarily high casualties; the CO therefore ordered all tanks back to hull-down positions, where they turned to the right in order to force the anti-tank front further south.

Again the tanks charged towards the enemy positions, but the leading vehicles hesitated. It was essential that the attack keep up its momentum; we had to achieve a break through, and could not wait for support to arrive. Lieutenant Michael took the lead, dragging the other tanks after him by force of example, and rolled on at top speed ignoring the fire which was concentrated on the leading vehicles. A few minutes seemed to last an eternity—but suddenly we were in among the excellently concealed enemy positions, with Soviets fighting desperately all round us. There were anti-tank guns to the right, to the left, and straight ahead. We rolled over them. The attack was irresistible. Panic-stricken Soviets attempted to retreat in all directions. We left the mopping-up to the Panzer-Grenadiers, and went storming on to the east.

Breathing freely once more, every crewman stared with strung-up nerves out into the darkness; despite the icy cold in the tanks everyone was bathed in perspiration. The CO reported: '1600 hrs, enemy position south of 147 penetrated. Presently no enemy contact. Moving east. Over.'

But how to move? We were still going across country, and had to find the right route among

A conversation which doomed the attempt to reach Stalingrad. Gen. Kirchner, commanding LVII Panzer Korps, ordered 6th Panzer to continue its advance from Wassiljewka; but Oberst von Huenersdorff demanded that his superior come personally to the bridgehead and assess the situation. Here Kirchner, in sidecap, is briefed by von Huenersdorff; behind them, in a Rumanian winter cap, is Oberst von Unrein, commander of 4th Pz-Gren.Regt.

SdKfz 251 half-tracks of the division photographed at Wassiljewka on the Myschkowa in late December 1942—just 48km from Stalingrad, and the furthest point of 6th Panzer's advance.

Tank fighting in southern Russia resembled desert warfare in some respects.

the ravines. The 'herd' broke up into a double column, with the CO close behind the spearhead—orientating oneself in the desert-like steppe was extremely difficult, and control was only possible if exercised from the front. We had to move 20km to the east, helped by the Pole Star exactly to our left. Firing was forbidden in order to avoid the enemy's attention. Only one thing mattered: winning the bridgehead.

With 12km to go to the Myschkowa we saw a dreamlike scene in the light of the newly risen moon. In a strong Soviet position the men of several infantry companies could be seen getting up, picking up their weapons, and staring silently at the queer-looking tank column. Hold your fire! As the bridge at this spot seemed unsuitable for tanks we used the ford beneath it. The first tank crossed and reached the far bank; then a second, a third, and a fourth. But the fifth tank—in which I rode with the CO—got track-slip half-way up the

opposite bank, and came to a halt. Reverse, and again with full throttle! Again, in vain.

Only 20 yards away to our right a platoon of Soviets were gathering on the bank. In the open hatches of our PzKpfw III the crew gripped their pistols and hand grenades. 'Once more—reverse! Now try a little further to the left!' But somehow the driver understood the order as 'right', and turned towards the watching Russians! Shouting and cursing seemed to make no difference—was the man deaf as well as blind? My heart was hammering frantically—'*Left!*' We were right in the middle of the dazed Russians, who clearly thought we were Soviets too. Not a word . . . the crew held their breath, while the driver made another attempt on the slope. The tracks began to slip again; then very slowly, an inch at a time, they got a grip. The tank crawled up the bank, and finally made the summit.

A little further on we met a Soviet motor column. They were obviously suspicious, and

Generalmajor Walter von Huenersdorff, 1898–1943. He rose from command of 11th Pz.Regt. in 1942 to command the division from February to July 1943. He was fatally wounded during the fighting near Belgorod in that month. A cadet in the 4th Hussars in 1915, he later served on Gen.Guderian's staff, and subsequently as Chief of Staff of Hoth's 3rd Panzer Army in 1941. He was posthumously awarded the Oakleaves to the Knight's Cross which he wears in this photograph; other visible decorations are the War Order of the German Cross in Gold, the Iron Cross 1st Class 1914–18 with 1939 bar, and the Tank Battle Badge, with the ribbons of the 2nd class Iron Cross 1914–18 and Winter 1941–42 Medal in his buttonhole.

after we had passed they fired an anti-tank gun after us. Then an enemy armoured car passed us—our last tank tried to ram it, but failed. We passed through a village, crowded with unsuspecting troops. Finally we reached the broad anti-tank ditch, and nearby lay the bridge over the Myschkowa. The bridge guards were taken by surprise, and once across the tanks fanned out into position, burning the last of their fuel.

Now the Soviets had woken up, and two T-34s opened fire. We silenced them, but not without loss: the gallant Lieutenant Michael was killed. The bridgehead was ours.

★   ★   ★

6th Panzer Division had approached within 48km (29 miles) of Stalingrad, but its impetus had been used up. The advance could not be maintained, and the Soviets built up a strong defence. For three days the division held its bridgehead in the hope that the Stalingrad garrison would break out and link up with them. The break-out never happened. On 23 December, deeply grieved, the division withdrew in obedience to an order to counter the new Soviet menace between the Don and the Donets. Here the enemy had renewed his offensive across the hard-frozen Don, penetrated the Italian 8th Army, encircled Millerovo, and threatened to cut off all German forces south of the Don and in the Caucasus. The mission to relieve Stalingrad had exceeded the division's available force.

Although 6th Panzer had started its mission with an entirely new allocation of fighting vehicles, they represented a weak force only. Available had been:

24 PzKpfw IV with the L/48 75mm gun (at least the equal of the 76.2mm gun of the Soviet T-34)

24 more L/48 75mm guns of the Anti-Tank Battalion

75 PzKpfw III with the L/60 50mm gun

30 PzKpfw III with the L/24 75mm gun

The short-barreled 75mm gun could penetrate 90mm of armour with its new HEAT ammunition at any normal range; but owing to its low muzzle velocity and its curved trajectory, its hit probability against tanks was very low. The 50mm gun was effective up to 800m (874 yards) against the

The heavy gun company of each Panzer-Grenadier regiment had six 150mm infantry howitzers on the 38(t) tank chassis (SdKfz 138/1), with a maximum range of 4,700m.

T-34, but the Soviet tank could 'kill' any German tank at ranges below 1,500m (1,640 yards). This situation, which could be circumvented only by the superior skill of the German crews, led to very high German losses and a rapid attrition of the division's strength in offensive operations—and it was to offensive operations that the division was committed! In four weeks of almost continuous operations 11th Panzer Regt. lost the bulk of its tanks, 35 officers and 400 men.

1943–45

During the battle between the Don and the Donets the division succeeded in effectively delaying the Soviet advance towards Rostov and Voroshilovgrad. The shrinking tank strength and the ever-improving Soviet anti-tank defences required new tactics. Against attack in superior numbers the only hope of success lay in the closest co-operation of all the mechanised arms. This was achieved by the improvisation of the 'Armoured battle group', comprising tanks, armoured infantry, self-propelled guns and other fighting vehicles, often from several different formations, gathered under the leadership of a single regimental commander. 'Panzerkampfgruppe von Huenersdorff' consisted of the armour of the 6th and 7th Panzer Divisions, reinforced by Army assault gun units. The remaining motorised units of these divisions were incapable of offensive operations, and were limited to static defence in

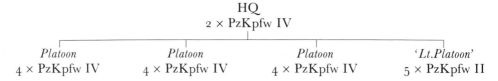

TABLE 7 — **Medium Tank Company,
11th Pz.Regt., 1938–43**

HQ
2 × PzKpfw IV

Platoon	*Platoon*	*Platoon*	*'Lt.Platoon'*
4 × PzKpfw IV	4 × PzKpfw IV	4 × PzKpfw IV	5 × PzKpfw II

NB: The PzKpfw IV was armed with the 75mm L/24 until the 1942 re-organisation, and thereafter with the 75mm L/48.

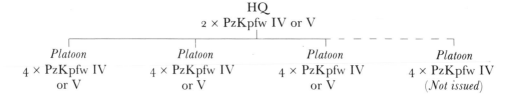

**Tank Company,
11th Pz.Regt., 1943–45**

HQ
2 × PzKpfw IV or V

Platoon	*Platoon*	*Platoon*	*Platoon*
4 × PzKpfw IV or V	4 × PzKpfw IV or V	4 × PzKpfw IV or V	4 × PzKpfw IV (*Not issued*)

NB: 1st Bn. normally had PzKpfw V Panthers, 2nd Bn. PzKpfw IVs.
The official establishment was four platoons of five tanks, but shortages led to the issue of only four per platoon. In addition a general reduction of about 10 per cent was ordered—'*Notsoll*'—and the fourth platoon disappeared.

the face of superior Soviet forces with heavy firepower and—due to the abundant supply of US vehicles—good off-road mobility. Despite its disadvantages the Panzerkampfgruppe concept was the only way to make successful counter-attacks, to regain key terrain features and to eliminate dangerous enemy forces.

In February 1943 6th Panzer Division, still in mobile defence, held a sector of the Donets in order to protect the withdrawal of 1st and 4th Panzer Armies towards a shortened front line. On

Among the new weapons issued to 6th Panzer in 1944 was the self-propelled 150mm howitzer, SdKfz 165 'Hummel'.

22 February—the beginning of a new phase—the division was ordered to counterattack from the Stalino area northwards, to outflank Soviet forces advancing towards the Dniepr. The manoeuvre succeeded. Striking northwards to the east of Kharkov as part of 4th Panzer Army, the division established contact with II SS Panzer Corps, thereby encircling Kharkov, which fell on 14 March. A few days later the west bank of the Donets was cleared of the enemy. The arrival of the spring thaw, with its heavy mud, then brought all operations to a standstill.

In April 1943 1st Bn., 11th Panzer Regt. left the division—without tanks or equipment—to prepare for re-equipment with the new PzKpfw V Panther tanks in Germany. For the next 20 months 6th Panzer Division's tank strength was limited to a regimental headquarters and one battalion equipped mainly with the PzKpfw IV.

From April to June the front opposite the division remained quiet. New equipment and replacements arrived; many men were sent on leave.

On 5 July Operation 'Citadel', a pincer movement, was launched against the flanks of the Soviet-held Kursk salient. Hitler was gambling for high stakes. 6th Panzer Division, as part of the southern pincer, penetrated 30km (19 miles) into the Russian salient during the first days of the fighting, exploiting a breach created by a neighbouring division. It was, however, slowed down badly by minefields. In this operation the gallant divisional commander, General von Huenersdorff, was fatally wounded—a serious loss for 6th Panzer.

From now on Germany had lost the initiative on the Eastern Front. As a result of the Allied landings in Sicily and of Italy's surrender the important SS Panzer divisions were withdrawn from Russia. This, in conjunction with the inevitable Soviet counterattack following the failure of the 'Citadel' offensive, led to a German withdrawal to the Dniepr. Unable to think in terms of strategy and the economy of forces, Hitler was obsessed with the static defence of fixed lines or fortified localities. This resulted in enormous losses of manpower and materiel in a succession of encirclements. Germany no longer had the troops available to cover the whole of her wide front lines, and had to rely on counter-attacks by her few mobile divisions to check the enemy. The overstretched Panzer divisions formed the core of this mobile defence, and their continuous commitment to battle led to rapid attrition.

Withdrawal from Russia

No member of the 6th Panzer Division spoke any longer of the *endsieg*—the final victory. The initiative had passed to the enemy once and for all. During the next few weeks of severe fighting, which sometimes reached its artillery lines, the decimated division repeatedly repulsed enemy attempts to penetrate or outflank its position, although contact with neighbouring formations was often lost. On 13 August the division held Kharkov against continuous attacks by superior Soviet armoured, infantry and heavy artillery forces. After ten days the division was allowed to fall back—the same day that 6th Panzer was able to proudly announce the destruction of its 1,500th enemy tank since the beginning of the Russian campaign.

Behind the front line lay the mighty Dniepr River, a suitable defensive line for the following

In the centre of this section of map is the railway bridge over the Dniepr at Kremenchug, over which Army Group South had to withdraw in late 1943. 6th Panzer was committed to repeated counterattacks north and south of this sector after withdrawing over the bridge on 25 September 1943. Note the poor quality of the map, overprinted with place names for German use.

winter. On 25 September 1943 the 6th Panzer Division crossed the river at Kremenchug. However, the thinly-spread German forces were unable to prevent Soviet crossings. The division, as part of Army reserve, was repeatedly committed to counterattacks on various sectors north and south of Kremenchug. The Soviet break through further north brought its 'armoured battle group' to Tcherkassy. In December the mud brought operations to a temporary halt, but not for long.

The Soviet winter offensive of late December 1943/early January 1944 created turmoil at several points along the front. Field Marshal von

Each armoured Panzer-Grenadier company received a section of two APCs with L/24 75mm guns (SdKfz 251/9) to replace towed 75mm anti-tank guns. Although its HEAT rounds penetrated 90mm of armour at any normal battle range, its hit probability was low due to its modest muzzle velocity.

Street fighting in Willkowischken, East Prussia, autumn 1944. Panzer-Grenadiers pass two captured anti-tank guns and a Schwimmwagen.

Manstein sent III Panzer Corps, spearheaded by 'Heavy Panzer Regiment Bäke', to the north. This *ad hoc* regiment, led by the then-CO of 11th Panzer Regt., comprised 34 Tiger tanks from 503rd Heavy Tank Bn., 47 Panthers from 2nd Bn., 23rd Panzer Regt., and a self-propelled artillery battalion. It succeeded in cutting off one head of the many-headed Soviet hydra, destroying 268 enemy tanks and 156 guns for light German losses. But the other heads were able to encircle 1st Panzer Army near Tcherkassy. Bäke led a raid which broke the Soviet ring, and as a result some 35,000 men in the Korsun Pocket were relieved.

The next Soviet thrusts towards Tarnopol cut a deep wedge in the German lines—another occasion on which Hitler's refusal to permit a withdrawal at the proper time had costly consequences. While the 6th Panzer Division, as part of 1st Panzer Army, attempted to stop the enemy in the north, another Soviet pincer struck further south and caught the whole army—the remnants of 18 divisions—in a pocket east of the Dniestr near Kamenets-Podolsk. The encircled German forces had to be supplied by air while awaiting relief by 4th Panzer Army, which was now led by General Raus, a former commander of 6th Panzer Division.

For this operation II SS Panzer Corps was transported to Galicia from Normandy, where it would be urgently required in June to resist the Allied landings. The corps was reinforced with 1st

Bn., 11th Panzer Regt., now returned to the front with its new Panthers. When the relief force launched its attack the encircled army was able to deceive the Soviets, who were awaiting a break-out attempt in the south. With the 6th Panzer Division as vanguard, and Panzerkampfgruppe Bäke as the tip of the spearhead, they broke out to the west. On 7 April 1944 6th Panzer Division and II SS Panzer Corps shook hands at Buczacz. The 200,000 men of 1st Panzer Army were extricated, and established a new front which remained static for some months. Even after the stabilisation of the situation Field Marshal Model did not at once allow the remnants of 6th Panzer Division to rest and recuperate. The division was employed in restoring and securing the front in Galicia for some weeks, and it was not until May that they were sent to north-west Germany for re-organisation and rebuilding.

During autumn 1944 production of the Panzerfaust hand-held anti-tank rocket projector allowed its widespread issue. Here a 'training round' is demonstrated to officers of the tank regiment.

The 1944 Re-organisation

According to the new table of organisation and equipment for the 'Panzer Division 44', the 6th Panzer should have been a powerful formation. However, the enormous losses of materiel since Stalingrad did not permit the full achievement of this goal, to say nothing of the poor quality and state of training of the replacements.

The 11th Panzer Regt. was still deprived of its 1st Bn.; the HQ Company received a platoon of 37mm anti-aircraft guns, and the 2nd Bn. received some 20mm quadruple AA mountings, but in the tank companies the establishment was reduced from 22 to 17 vehicles each.

The mechanisation of the Panzer-Grenadier regiments was hardly improved. Only the HQ and 2nd Bn. of 114th Pz-Gren.Regt. were equipped with APCs, the 1st Bn. being only motorised. A 3rd Bn. was formed without authority, an improvisation to give the regimental commander two battalions even when the armoured battalion was removed for service with the Panzerkampfgruppe. This 'illegal' battalion included a volunteer Cossack mounted squadron. The fire-support of the divisional infantry was improved by the issue to each of the regimental gun companies of six self-propelled 150mm infantry howitzers on Skoda 38(t) chassis (Sd.Kfz.138/1). The seven APC-

---

TABLE 8   **Panzer-Grenadier Company,
6th Panzer Division, 1944–45**

In principle organisation of armoured infantry at the end of the war differed little from the motorised rifle regiments of 1937–38. Although Panzer-Grenadiers were supposed to be capable of fighting mounted or dismounted they were still organised 'in threes', i.e. three rifle platoons in each of three companies in a battalion. In practice the platoon now had only three rather than four sections, but a fourth sub-unit was evolved for fire support. The already impressive firepower achieved by pre-war rifle regiments, with their double allocation of machine guns, was further improved by the issue of more machine guns with heavy mountings for sustained fire in the dismounted rôle, and by the weapons mounted on the transport vehicles of the sections. The development of new tactics and the firepower of additional support weapons rendered the machine gun less important than the mortar, and required decentralisation of weaponry. This was partly a result of the permanent shortage of tanks and artillery. The resulting unit was very self-sufficient, but complex:

HQ
1 × SdKfz 251/17
(20mm AA gun)

Platoon	Platoon	Platoon	Heavy Weapons Platoon
1 × SdKfz 251/17 (20mm AA gun)	1 × SdKfz 251/17 (20mm AA gun)	1 × SdKfz 251/17 (20mm AA gun)	3 × SdKfz 251/17 (20mm AA gun, plus MGs on heavy ground mountings)
4 × SdKfz 251/1 (10 or 11 riflemen)	4 × SdKfz 251/1 (10 or 11 riflemen)	4 × SdKfz 251/1 (10 or 11 riflemen)	2 × SdKfz 251/2 (mounted 81mm mortar) 2 × SdKfz 251/9 (75mm L/24 gun)

This company was supported:
At battalion level by six additional 75mm L/24 guns (Sd.Kfz.251/9) and four 120mm mortars, all mounted on half-tracks, and in some cases by quad-20mm mountings (Sd.Kfz.7/1) and 28cm-rocket-launcher vehicles; and *at regimental level* by six 150mm SP infantry howitzers (Sd.Kfz.138/1).

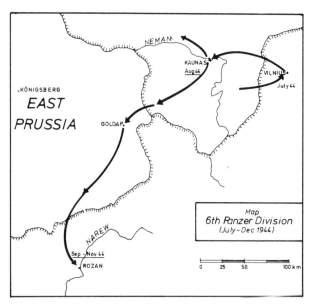

Panzer-Grenadiers in defensive positions, supported by the fire of Nebelwerfer multibarrel rocket-launchers, here using incendiary rounds.

mounted 20mm anti-aircraft guns which were authorised for each rifle company did not materialise, however.

The 41st Tank Destroyer Bn. was equipped with two companies of 75mm Panzerjäger IV self-propelled guns (SdKfz 162), and one towed 75mm company. The 76th Artillery Regt. comprised, as before, one battalion with self-propelled 105mm (Wespe) and 150mm (Hummel) howitzers, one battalion with towed 105mm light field howitzers, and one battalion with towed 150mm medium field howitzers.

All fighting units were re-organised so as to form a supply company per battalion. By this organisation the strength of the division was reduced by 2,000 men.

Frontier Defence in East Prussia

During their summer 1944 offensive in White Russia the Soviets succeeded in driving deep wedges into the German front lines, destroying most of Army Group Centre and endangering 3rd Panzer Army in Lithuania. This Army protected the eastern frontier of East Prussia and the Baltic states, where Army Group North was based. The Red Army encircled Vilna, and the 6th Panzer Division was rushed to its relief in July. De-training at Kaunas on 12 July, the division went into action immediately and succeeded in breaking the ring and extricating 5,000 men.

An attack to the north was planned in order to counter the Soviet threat to the supply base and land communications of Army Group North, but fell short when the Soviets launched a new drive towards the East Prussian frontier in August. The division helped to counter this thrust.

On 26 August 6th Panzer was sent to the Narew River in northern Poland as Army reserve for the 2nd Army. Here it fought in mobile defence to prevent an enemy break through to southern East Prussia. The divisional battle groups counter-attacked again and again in support of the worn-out infantry divisions. On 14 October 2nd Bn., 11th Panzer Regt. was cut off by superior enemy forces, but managed to fight its way out.

In October the division celebrated its fifth birthday, and reported a total of 2,378 Soviet tanks destroyed since June 1941. It had no rest until November, when it was relieved and received replacements. Since July 1st Bn., Panzer Regt. 'Grossdeutschland' had been detached to the 6th Panzer Division; this unit was now replaced by 1st Bn., 11th Panzer Regt. which returned to its parent division at last. After thorough training with Panther tanks in Germany and France it had been attached to 8th Panzer Division in March 1944, and had suffered heavy casualties. It had been brought up to strength again at Grafenwöhr camp before rejoining its parent division, with the exception of its 4th Company. This sub-unit became well known in the West; interestingly, it had been equipped at Magdeburg depot with captured Sherman tanks and was later committed to the Ardennes fighting near Malmedy as part of the so-called 150th Panzer Brigade, which also included other units dressed in Allied uniforms.

To Hungary

Beginning on 8 December 1944, 6th Panzer Division was transported to Hungary. Hitler had

Blurred but 'atmospheric' photographs of an early-morning counterattack in East Prussia late in 1944, launched by 'Panzerkampfgruppe Schmidt' the division's armoured battle-group, named after the then-commander of 11th Pz.Regt. with Panther and PzKpfw IV tanks and armoured infantry in SdKfz 251 half-tracks.

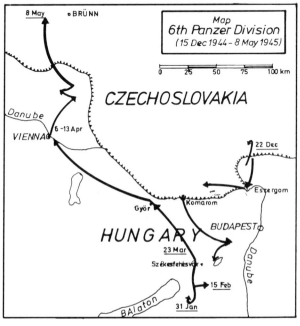

Map
6th Panzer Division
(15 Dec 1944 – 8 May 1945)

0   25   50   75   100 km

8 May   ● BRÜNN

CZECHOSLOVAKIA

Danube

VIENNA   6–13 Apr

22 Dec

Esztergom

Győr   Komárom

BUDAPEST

HUNGARY

23 Mar

Székesfehérvár

15 Feb

Balaton   31 Jan

Danube

decided to concentrate more German forces there when the collapse of Rumania exposed Hungary to the advance of Soviet forces. There was a fear that Hungary, site of the last oilfields and bauxite mines available to Germany, might be tempted to surrender. When the division de-trained north of Lake Balaton two separate Soviet armies were approaching Budapest, one north of the Danube and the other south.

Attempts to support the German defences against both claws of this pincer required the splitting of 6th Panzer: the Panzerkampfgruppe remained in the south while the motorised element fought at Esztergom. This enforced dispersal of strength underlines the critical situation on the Eastern Front at a time when German forces were also heavily committed to the Ardennes offensive in the West. 6th Panzer Division was able to delay the Soviet advance but unable to prevent the encirclement of Budapest at Christmas. In January the division held a sector in the mountains west of the city; it found itself cut off on several occasions, but each time managed to fight its way out, destroying many enemy tanks and guns. During the concentration of the mobile forces near Székesfehésvar for an attempt to relieve the siege of Budapest, the Red Army launched a new offensive from Baranov which frustrated the German counter-stroke. The division was severely weakened in continuous fighting against superior enemy forces.

After the failure of all attempts to break through to Budapest, or to break out from inside the encirclement, Hitler ordered another futile operation beginning on 6 March 1945. An attack by 6th Panzer on the north bank of Lake Verence bogged down in muddy going in front of stubborn Soviet defences. On 16 March the Red Army launched their well-planned final offensive. The division managed to fall back to the Austrian frontier, east of Lake Neusiedl, at the last minute.

The last stand

While in western Germany the Ruhr Pocket was slamming closed on large German forces, the 6th Panzer Division was ordered to the defence of Vienna, under II SS Panzer Corps. During early April the division slowly fell back in order to minimise damage to the ancient city. 6th Panzer was to hold the Reichsbrücke, the last bridge across the Danube, essential for the retreat of all German forces south of the river. All enemy attempts to capture the bridge failed, including air strikes and, on 13 April, an assault boat attack. On 14 April the German forces finally gave up

Most Panzer units originated in the old cavalry branch; this monument to 7th Company, 11th Pz.Regt. at Paderborn traces its descent from Reiter-Regt.15, which itself traced its identity to the 4th Cuirassier Regt. of the Imperial German and Prussian Armies.

Vienna, and 6th Panzer Division withdrew north of Brünn. On 7 May it was holding a sector north of that town when it was decided to move west in order to surrender to Patton's 3rd US Army rather than to the Soviets. All tanks, armoured vehicles and weapons were blown up.

The attempt succeeded, but was to be in vain: the US Army handed over most captured members of 6th Panzer Division to the Red Army, and they were held in captivity in Russia until 1955—the same year in which the new German Bundeswehr was established. 6th Panzer Division had ceased to exist, after six years of gallant fighting in accordance with their duty as soldiers.